DICTIONARY, GLOSSARY AND THESAURUS: HOW TO USE THEM?

LANGUAGE REFERENCE BOOK GRADE 4 | CHILDREN'S ESL BOOKS

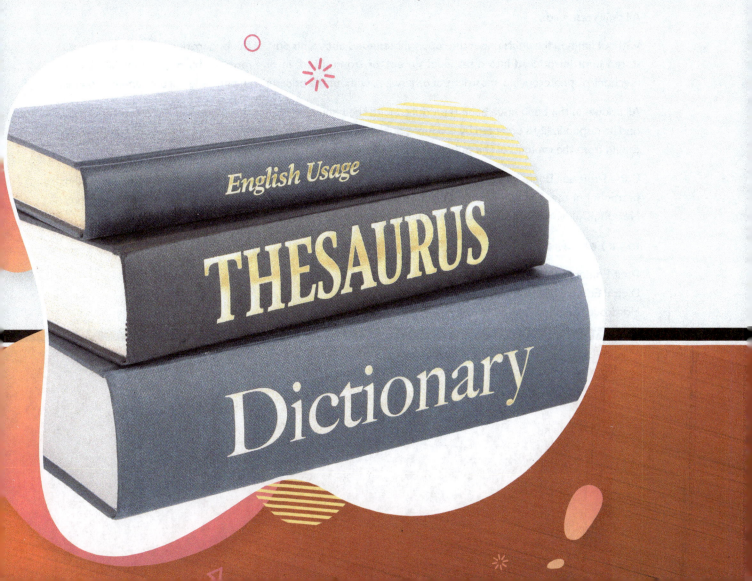

First Edition, 2021

Published in the United States by Speedy Publishing LLC, 40 E Main Street, Newark, Delaware 19711 USA.

© 2021 Baby Professor Books, an imprint of Speedy Publishing LLC

All rights reserved.

Without limiting the rights under the copyright reserved above, no part of this publication may be reproduced, stored in or introduced into a retrieval system, or transmitted, in any form, or by any means (electronic, mechanical, photocopying, recording, or otherwise), without the prior written permission of the copyright owner.

All images in this book have been reproduced with the knowledge and prior consent of the artists concerned, and no responsibility is accepted by producer, publisher, or printer for any infringement of copyright or otherwise arising from the contents of this publication.

Baby Professor Books are available at special discounts when purchased in bulk for industrial and sales-promotional use. For details contact our Special Sales Team at Speedy Publishing LLC, 40 E Main Street, Newark, Delaware 19711 USA. Telephone (888) 248-4521 Fax: (210) 519-4043.

10 9 8 7 6 * 5 4 3 2 1

Print Edition: 9781541953741
Digital Edition: 9781541956742
Hardcover Edition: 9781541980624

See the world in pictures. Build your knowledge in style.
www.speedypublishing.com

TABLE OF CONTENTS

WHAT IS A DICTIONARY? 9
    The Dictionary Listing 12
    What Is the History of Dictionaries? 15
    How Do You Use a Dictionary? 19

WHAT IS A THESAURUS? 23
    What Is the History of Thesaurus? 29
    How Do You Use a Thesaurus? 33
    Be Careful Using the Thesaurus 37

WHAT IS A GLOSSARY? 43
    What Is the History of Glossaries? 49
    How Do You Use a Glossary? 50
    Online Versions 54

SUMMARY 59

An atlas provides us with information about different places in the world.

The bookshelves in your classroom or your school library include some books that are called reference books[1] because we refer to them to find specific information that we need. An atlas, for example, provides us with information about different places in the world.

---

1 Reference – A source of information that you can refer to when seeking knowledge.

An almanac, another type of reference book, gives us information about events of a certain year. Included in these books are language reference books such as dictionaries and thesauruses. In this book, we will take a look at three examples of reference books - the dictionary, thesaurus and glossary - to see how they began and how students like you can use them.

A good dictionary can help you understand your subject better and improve your communication.

English Usage

THESAURUS

Dictionary

WHAT IS A DICTIONARY?

One of the first pieces of information that you will see in a dictionary is the correct spelling of the word.

Many people think that the dictionary is the book to refer to when you don't know how to spell a word. That is true, but there is much more to dictionaries than that. A dictionary is a book that is a collection of all the words in a certain language. There is one listing for each word. Within the listing, you will find quite a bit of information about the word. One of the first pieces of information that you will see is the correct spelling of the word, as well as all the acceptable alternate spellings.

THE DICTIONARY LISTING

After the correct spelling of the word, you will find the pronunciation of the word, written using **phonetic**[2] symbols. Next is the definition of the word. If the word has more than one definition, all of them will be included. The dictionary entry will also include the part or parts of speech of the word – whether it is a noun, verb, adverb, pronoun, adjective, preposition, or article. You should also find additional information about the word, such as the language of origin, variations, as well as words that mean the same and words that mean the opposite.

---

[2] Phonetic – A written representation of spoken speech.

terminology

[tur-*muh*-nol-*uh*-jee]

noun, plural 'terminologies'
1. the system of terms belonging or peculiar to a science, art, or specialized subject; nomenclature.
2. the science of terms, as in particular sciences or arts.

Word Origin and History for 'terminology'

1, from German Terminologie (1786), a hybrid ... by C.G. Schütz of Jena, from Medieval ... word, expression" (see terminu... ...with, a speaking of...

> After the correct spelling of the word, you will find the pronunciation of the word, written using phonetic symbols.

A Table Alphabeticall, contayning and teaching the true writing and vnderstanding of hard vsuall English words, borrowed from the Hebrew, Greeke, Latine, or French, &c.

the Interpretation thereof by
the English words, ga...
...nefit and help of all...

> Table Alphabeticali was an actual dictionary with both spellings and definitions.

WHAT IS THE HISTORY OF DICTIONARIES?

Some of the earliest English dictionaries, written in the Middle Ages, were actually translation tools that contained words of English and another language, such as French. One of the first true English dictionaries, compiled in 1582 by Richard Mulcaster, was basically a spelling guide with no definitions. Robert Cawdrey's 1604 book, called *Table Alphabeticali*, was an actual dictionary with both spellings and definitions, although it contained only about 2,500 words.

Another dictionary, published about fifty years later by Thomas Blount, included more than 10,000 words. While the Oxford English Dictionary, which was first published in 1884, has become the foremost English dictionary, the Webster Dictionary of 1806 was the first American dictionary. Like all good reference books, dictionaries are regularly updated to include new words and additional meanings.

Like all good reference books, dictionaries are regularly updated to include new words and additional meanings.

Dictionaries are arranged in alphabetical order so you can find the listings under the first letter of the word.

HOW DO YOU USE A DICTIONARY?

How you use a dictionary depends first on why you need to use it. If you need it to learn how a word is spelled, you will start with the first letter of the word. Dictionaries are arranged in alphabetical order so you can find the listings under the first letter of the word and, by sounding out the word, do your best to find it in the listings.

If you want to know the meaning of a word, you simply find it in the alphabetical listing and read the definition or definitions in the entry. If you are not sure how a word is used, look for abbreviations, like "v.", "n.", or "adj.", that will tell you if the word is a verb, noun, or adjective.

English

[ing-glish *or, often,* -lish]

adjective

1. of, relating to, or characteristic of England or its inhabitants, institutions, etc.
2. belonging or relating to, or spoken or written in, the English language: a high-school English class.

noun

the people of England collectively, especially as distinguished from the Scots, Welsh, and Irish Germanic language of the British Isles and standard also in the U. Commonwealth,

> If you are not sure how a word is used, look for abbreviations, like "v.", "n.", or "adj.", that will tell you if the word is a verb, noun, or adjective.

English Usage

THESAURUS

Dictionary

WHAT IS A THESAURUS?

There are a lot of words in the English language and many words mean roughly the same thing as other words.

There are a lot of words in the English language and many words mean roughly the same thing as other words. To find words with similar meanings, you can look in a thesaurus. Like a dictionary, a thesaurus is a language reference book. Within the pages of a thesaurus, however, you will find synonyms and antonyms of words.

A word or phrase that means the same thing as another word, or has a meaning that is very close to that of another word, is called a synonym. For example, "big" and "large" are synonyms for each other. An antonym is a word or phrase that means the opposite of another word. "Little", for example, is the antonym of "big".

An antonym is a word or phrase that means the opposite of another word. "Little", for example, is the antonym of "big".

Dr. Peter Roget was a British physician, natural theologian, and a lexicographer.

WHAT IS THE HISTORY OF THESAURUS?

Dr. Peter Roget, who was an English physician and mathematician rather than a writer or **linguist**[3], kept a collection of synonyms for his own personal hobby and to help him with his own writing. His list was handy, and friends and family often asked if they could reference it for their own writing projects.

---

3   Linguist – A person who is an expert in languages.

In the early 1840s, after much encouragement from his friends, he quit his job as a doctor to devote his full attention to expanding and organizing his list of synonyms. In 1852, he published his *Roget's Thesaurus*, a reference guide that has been in print ever since. You may wonder about the word "thesaurus" itself. Roget selected this word for his collection because it means "treasure" in Greek.

The word "thesaurus" means "treasure" in Greek.

> Like a dictionary, the entries in a thesaurus are listed alphabetically.

HOW DO YOU USE A THESAURUS?

Like a dictionary, the entries in a thesaurus are listed alphabetically. If you realize you are using the same word multiple times in your writing, you may want to consult a thesaurus to find another word that means the same thing. If the word you are overusing is "big", for example, you just need to look under the "B" section in the thesaurus and find the word "big". Within the entry, you will see a host of other words, including "large, huge, massive, and enormous."

If what you need is a word that means the opposite of "big", you can find that too. Under the list of antonyms for "big", you will find several words, including "little, tiny, small, and minuscule."

You can see antonyms of words in a thesaurus.

Be careful in using the thesaurus as some words can have slight variations in meanings.

BE CAREFUL USING THE THESAURUS

Some students, upon discovering the thesaurus, decide to spice up their writing by replacing many of their own words with synonyms they find in the thesaurus. That can lead to some comical and misleading sentences. Words that are synonymous with each other can have slight variations in meanings that can totally change your writing if you are not aware of them.

For example, you may want to find a different way to say "big sister" so you look up "big" in the thesaurus and come across a synonym for "big" … "burly". But when you change "big sister" to "burly sister", you have changed the meaning of your phrase. Instead of referring to an older sibling, you are now describing your sister as muscular, bulky, and as having an intimidating mannish appearance.

When you change "big sister" to "burly sister", you have changed the meaning of your phrase.

Taking a sentence from another source and changing a few words by substituting in their synonyms is still considered plagiarism.

Another word of warning about thesaurus use… it should not be a tool to help you plagiarize or copy another person's words. Some students believe that they can take a sentence from another source, change a few words by substituting in their synonyms, and turn the work in as their own original writing. That is still considered **plagiarism**[4].

---

4   Plagiarism – The act of copying or closely copying the words or ideas of someone else and attempting to pass them off as your own original words or ideas.

English Usage

THESAURUS

Dictionary

WHAT IS A GLOSSARY?

Generally, non-fiction books, textbooks, and technical guides may have glossaries.

A glossary is different from a dictionary and a thesaurus in that it is not a separate reference guide but is found within certain books. Generally, non-fiction books, textbooks, and technical guides may have glossaries, but most novels do not.

A glossary is a guide, typically found at the back of a book, that lists the words and definitions that are located within the book. It is a tool to help people to understand the words and terms in the context of that book so that they have a clearer grasp of the information.

A glossary is a tool to help people to understand the words and terms in the context of that book so that they have a clearer grasp of the information.

Glossaries were common throughout medieval Europe and appeared in a number of religious books dating back farther than 800 CE.

WHAT IS THE HISTORY OF GLOSSARIES?

Glossaries were common throughout medieval Europe and appeared in a number of religious books dating back farther than 800 CE. Since Latin was the language of the Christian church but was not the common spoken language of the people, books often contained a glossary, or list of words so that readers of the book could understand its meaning. Today, we think of "gloss" as meaning "shiny, or polished" but another meaning of the word is "to explain or define, or to provide additional information".

HOW DO YOU USE A GLOSSARY?

When you are reading a textbook or another kind of book, you may notice that some of the unfamiliar words are in bold type. This is often a clue that the book contains a glossary in the back and that you can find the definition of the unfamiliar word listed there. In most cases, a book's glossary is a single list that appears in alphabetical order. It is easy to locate the word you need.

When you are reading a textbook or another kind of book, you may notice that some of the unfamiliar words are in bold type.

CHAPTER ON[E]

...the woods was a wide causeway... ...it. Both were so dirty... ...unrecognisable as human... ...that seemed unnaturally... ...that plaster...

> Occasionally, you may come across a book that has its glossary divided by chapters.

Occasionally, you may come across a book that has its glossary divided by chapters. You will need to know what chapter you are reading to look up the unfamiliar word, but it is set up to be clear and easy to use.

ONLINE VERSIONS

Today, more and more of the books and articles that you read are in digital format rather than on paper. That doesn't mean that we no longer have a need for dictionaries, thesauruses, and glossaries. It just means that these language reference books have evolved to keep up with current technology.

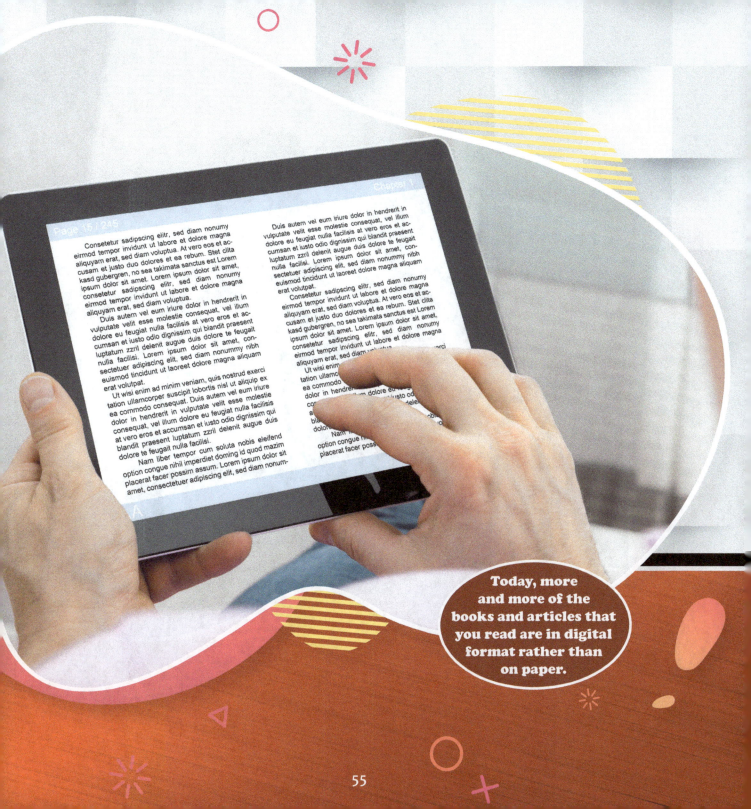

Today, more and more of the books and articles that you read are in digital format rather than on paper.

You can access several dictionaries and thesauruses through the internet.

You can access several dictionaries and thesauruses through the internet. In most word processing programs, you can look up a word to get its correct spelling, find its definition, and see its synonyms. If you are reading a book on a tablet or an article on a laptop, there are tools available for you to access dictionaries and glossaries with just a simple click.

English Usage

THESAURUS

Dictionary

SUMMARY

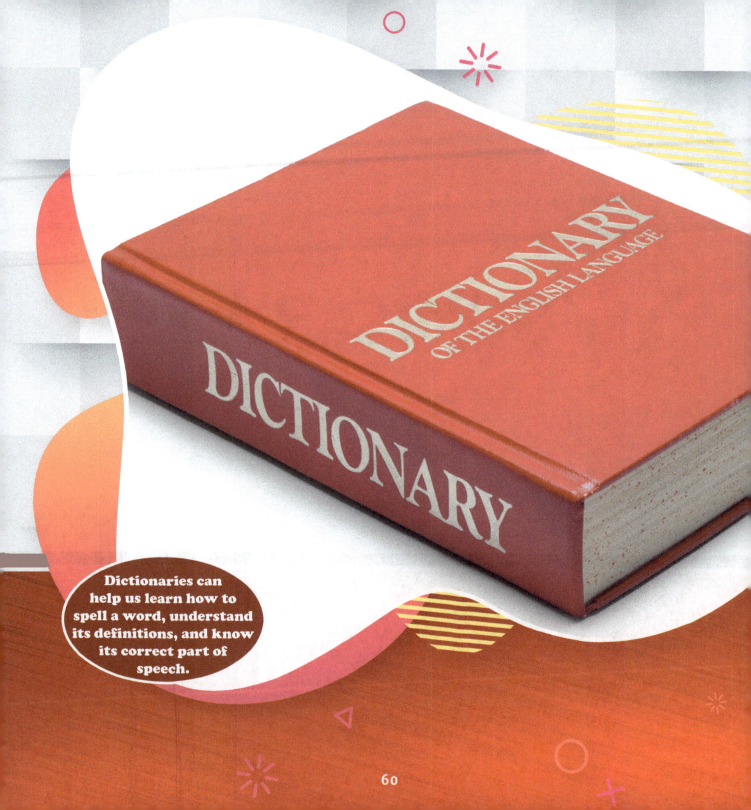

Dictionaries can help us learn how to spell a word, understand its definitions, and know its correct part of speech.

There are tools called reference books that help us to be better readers and better writers. Dictionaries can help us learn how to spell a word, understand its definitions, and know its correct part of speech.

Thesauruses provide us with a list of synonyms and antonyms so we can find other words that mean the same thing or words that have an opposite meaning.

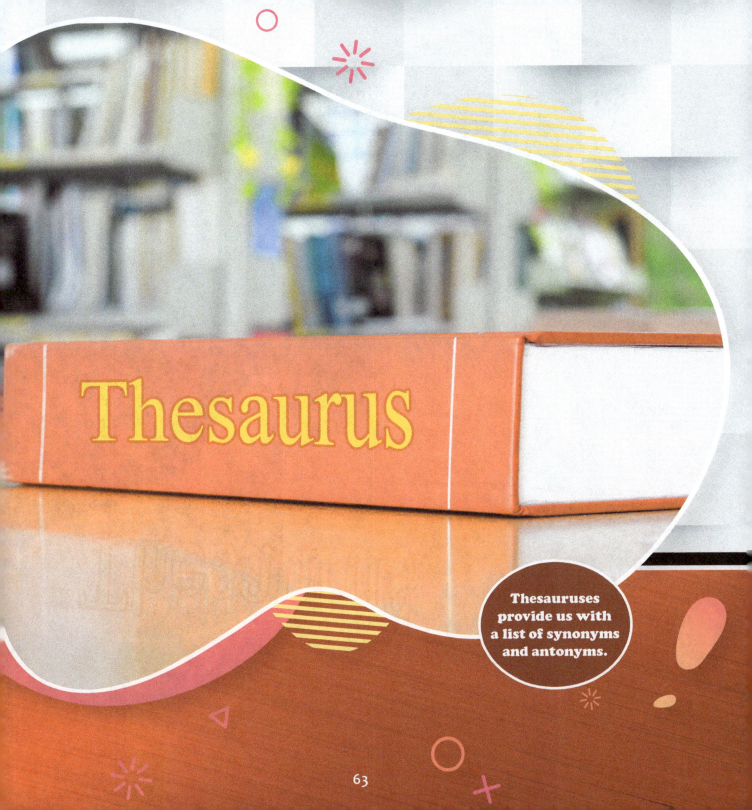

Thesauruses provide us with a list of synonyms and antonyms.

All of these language reference books are designed to help students to become better writers.

Glossaries, which are usually found at the back of books, help us understand the specific words that are used in that book. All of these language reference books are designed to help students to become better writers and to be able to understand the material they are reading.

Now that you know how to use dictionaries, glossaries, and thesauruses, you should plan a visit to your school library to see the other reference books that are there, such as atlases, almanacs, and **encyclopedias**[5].

---

5 Encyclopedia – A set of books containing brief articles about a wide variety of topics, arranged in alphabetical order.

Plan a visit to your school library to see the other reference books that are there, such as atlases, almanacs, and encyclopedias.

The Library of Congress was founded in 1800, making it the oldest federal cultural institution in the US.